Alfred's Premier Piano Express

Dennis Alexander, Gayle Kowalchyk, E. L. Lancaster, Victoria McArthur & Martha Mier

FOREWORD

Alfred's *Premier Piano Express* Christmas Book 4 includes familiar Christmas pieces that reinforce concepts included in the All-In-One Accelerated Course, Book 4 of *Premier Piano Express*. The music continues the strong pedagogical focus of the course while providing the enjoyment of playing familiar music during the Christmas season.

Christmas Book 4 is not correlated page by page with *Premier Piano Express*, Book 4. Pieces are arranged in progressive order of difficulty with the easiest pieces first, though it is not necessary to progress straight through the book.

Allowing students to study music they enjoy during the Christmas season is highly motivating. Consequently, reading and rhythm skills often improve greatly when studying holiday music. The authors hope that the music in Christmas Book 4 brings hours of enjoyment to this festive season. Merry Christmas!

D0841808

CONTENTS

Printed in USA.

ISBN-10: 1-4706-4076-7
ISBN-13: 978-1-4706-4076-7

Produced by
Alfred Music
P.O. Box 10003
Van Nuys, CA 91410-0003

alfred.com

Cover Photo:
Christmas Wreath: © Getty Images / Oksana Ariskina / EyeEm

Jingle Bells

James S. Pierpont came from a wealthy Boston family. In 1857, he wrote a song intended for Sunday School children to sing on Thanksgiving. Though written for that holiday, the jingle-bell rhythm was so appealing that it soon became one of the best-known Christmas songs in the world. Pierpont wrote many songs, but is remembered for **Jingle Bells.**

James S. Pierpont

What Child Is This?

This beautiful carol uses the 16th-century melody of the English tune Greensleeves. Originally, the song was played rather fast, for dancing, but its attractive melody became apparent when it was performed slowly. William Chatterton Dix, an insurance man and poet, wrote the words in 1865.

Words by William Chatterton Dix
Music: "Greensleeves" (16th century)

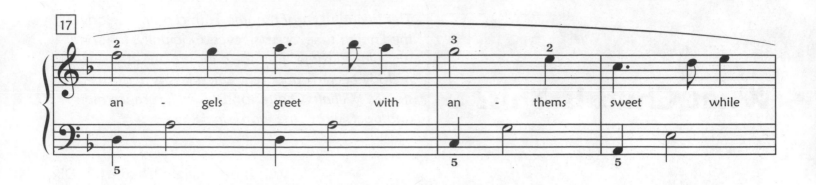

an - gels greet with an - thems sweet while

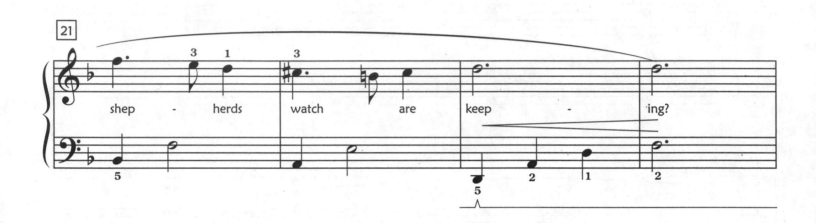

shep - herds watch are keep - ing?

This, this is Christ the King, whom

simile

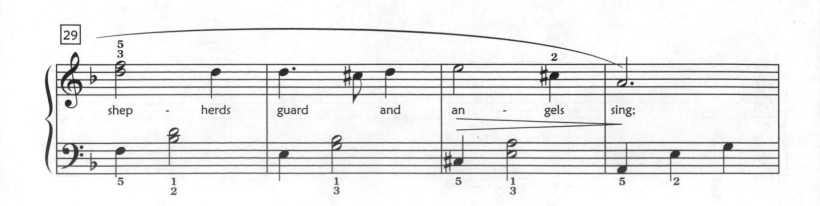

shep - herds guard and an - gels sing;

haste,   haste   to   bring   Him   laud,   the   Babe,

mf

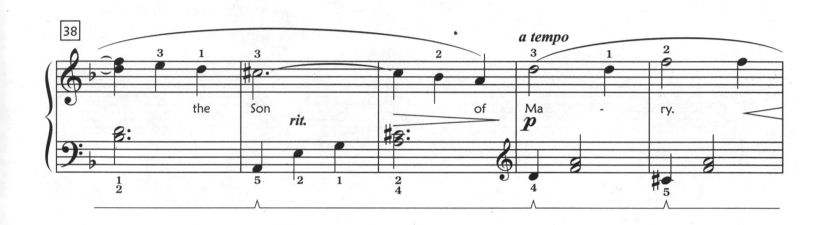

the   Son   of   Ma   -   ry.

rit.   *a tempo*   *p*

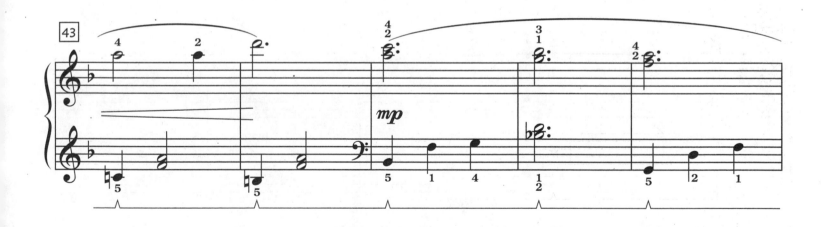

mp

poco rit.   *p*

It Came Upon the Midnight Clear

Unitarian minister Edmund Hamilton Sears wrote the words of **It Came Upon the Midnight Clear** in 1849 in Lancaster, Massachusetts. His words are often sung to a tune by Arthur Sullivan (of Gilbert & Sullivan fame), but the more familiar melody was written in 1850 by Boston-born composer Richard S. Willis (1819–1900). Willis was a student of Felix Mendelssohn.

Words by Edmund H. Sears
Music by Richard S. Willis

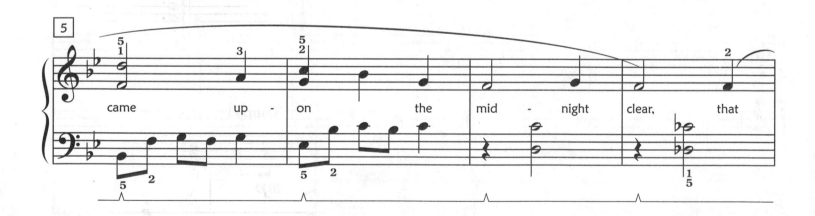

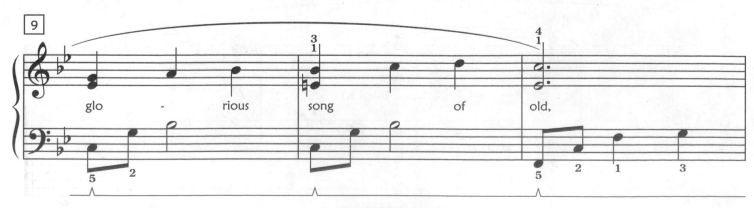

from an - gels bend - ing

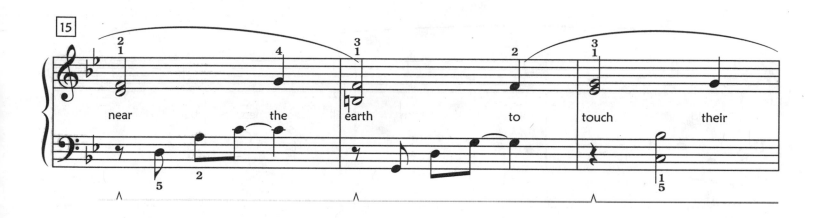

near the earth to touch their

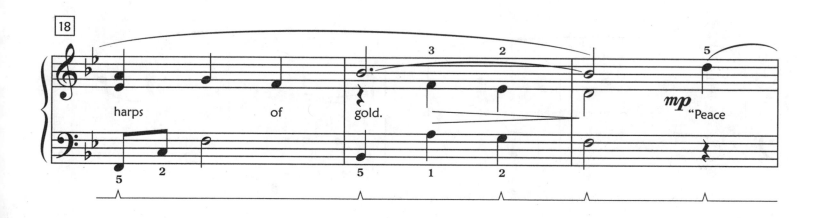

harps of gold. *mp* "Peace

on the earth good - will to men, from

heav'n's all gra - cious King." The

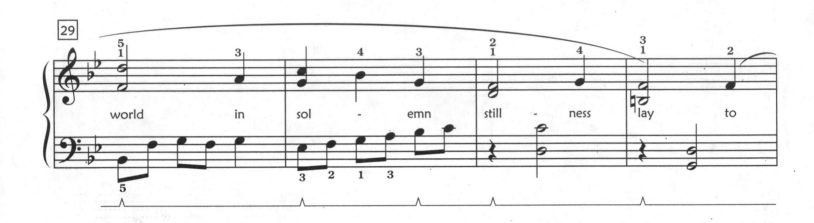

world in sol - emn still - ness lay to

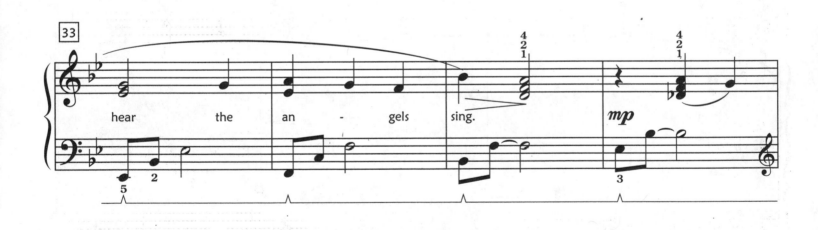

hear the an - gels sing. *mp*

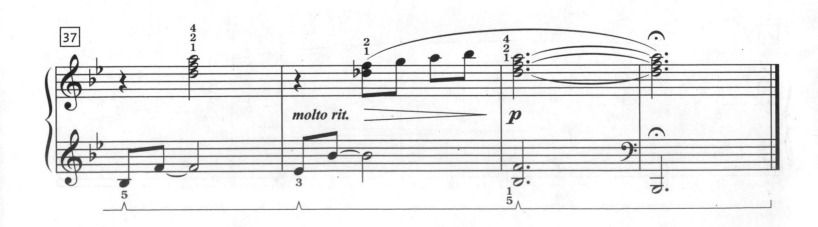

molto rit. *p*

March
(from *The Nutcracker*)

March is from Tchaikovsky's famous 1892 ballet, The Nutcracker. *The first scene of the ballet takes place on Christmas Eve at the Silberhaus home, which has just been decorated for Christmas. The family is gathered around the beautiful Christmas tree as fanciful dancers perform to the March.*

Peter Ilyich Tchaikovsky

Gesù Bambino
(The Infant Jesus)

*Italian-born composer Pietro Yon (1886–1943) won many prizes for performing on the piano and on the organ before coming to the United States in 1907. Later, Yon became the organist at St. Patrick's Cathedral in New York City. Among his many choral and organ works, **Gesù Bambino**, composed in 1917, is the best known. In this work, he cleverly combines an original melody with the traditional Adeste Fideles.*

English Lyrics by Frederick H. Martens
Music and Italian Lyrics by Pietro A. Yon

Silent Night

In 1818, just before Christmas, Father Joseph Mohr noticed that his church organ was damaged and unplayable. He needed something to sing on Christmas Eve, so he quickly wrote some lyrics and gave them to his organist, Franz Grüber. Mohr asked Grüber to compose a simple melody that could be accompanied by a few guitar chords. **Silent Night** *was the result of their collaboration and has been translated into over 44 languages.*

Franz Grüber

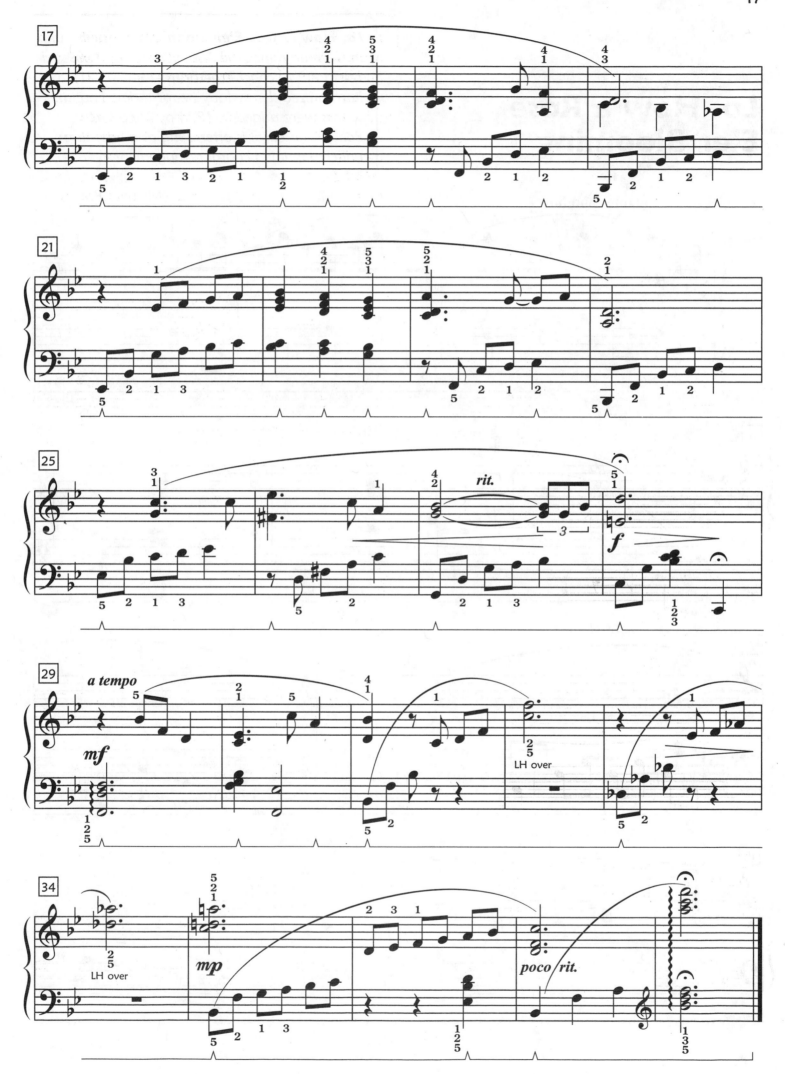

Lo, How a Rose E'er Blooming

Lo, How a Rose E'er Blooming has been sung in Germany since the 16th century. In 1609, composer Michael Praetorius (1571–1621) harmonized the melody heard today. English words were added in 1894 by Theodore Baker. This carol is often sung as a haunting unaccompanied choral arrangement.

Music by Michael Praetorius

Deck the Halls

*Originally called **Deck the Hall** (with no s), this Welsh melody is from the 16th century. The original Welsh words were about New Year's night; the familiar words printed here date from the 1880s. In many versions the "fa la la" is played by a harp. Even today, the holly's red berries and green leaves mentioned in the carol are traditional colors of the holiday.*

Traditional Welsh Carol

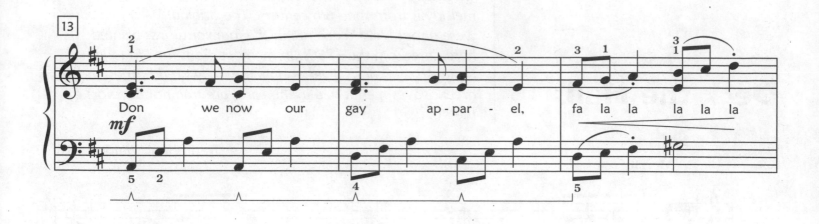

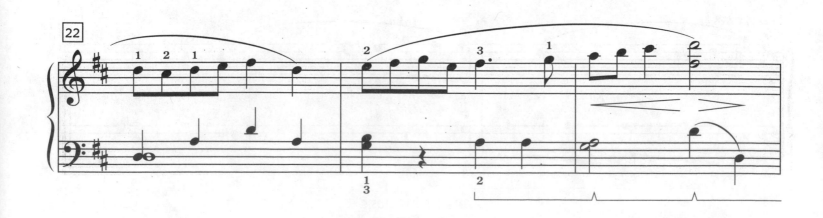

We Wish You a Merry Christmas

In the late 1830s in England, groups of carolers, called waits, would stroll through the streets of London, singing for a bit of pudding or a cup of good cheer. **We Wish You a Merry Christmas** was originally a "waits' carol" and became very popular in the mid-19th century.

Traditional English Carol

hap - py New Year! *mp*

Waltz of the Flowers

(from *The Nutcracker*)

The premiere performance of Tchaikovsky's *The Nutcracker* ballet in St. Petersburg in 1892 was not a success. But the music was so beautiful that Tchaikovsky selected eight of the more popular pieces and put them together to create The Nutcracker Suite. ***Waltz of the Flowers*** *is one of the favorites from the suite. The flower dancers have a beautiful, graceful scene in Act Two of the ballet.*

Peter Ilyich Tchaikovsky

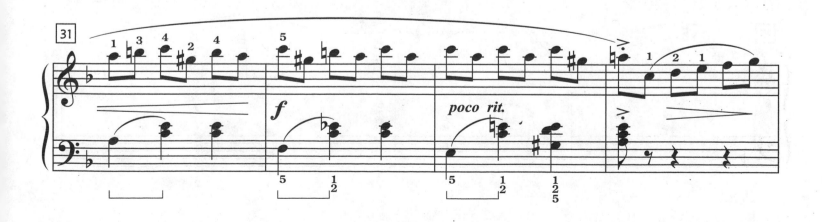

Still, Still, Still

Still, Still, Still is a traditional Austrian Christmas song from the collection Salzburger Volkslieder (Salzburg Folk Songs) of 1819. The beautiful melody became particularly popular in the United States following the release of a version by the music group Mannheim Steamroller.

Traditional Austrian Carol

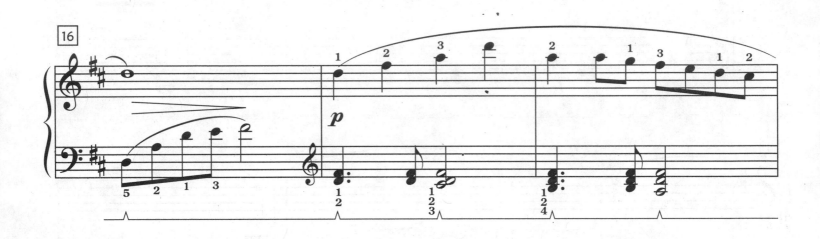

Auld Lang Syne

***Auld Lang Syne** is not strictly a Christmas song but it is traditionally sung on New Year's Eve. The tradition seems to have begun in 1929 when Guy Lombardo, a popular orchestra leader, played it over the radio. Since then, it has been played every New Year's Eve on radio and television. The song originated in Scotland, and the title means "Old Long Ago."*

Words by Robert Burns
Traditional Scottish Melody